LETTING GO
AND
LIVING FREE

Life Application
Journal

This journal belongs to:

INTRO

You were created by God to live in freedom, abundance and victory every day of your life.

In fact, that's a promise Jesus made to every person who believes in Him. He said in John 10:10, *I came that they may have and enjoy life, and have it in abundance [to the full, till it overflows].*

Yet what I've discovered is that oftentimes, most believers only end up halfway to the point of having abundant life. They start out enthusiastic for God and His Word, but at some point, they find themselves living in survival mode, burdened by the pressures of daily life.

But Jesus didn't die for us to live this way.

He wants you to really enjoy your life...to be passionate about what He's passionate about, excited to grow in your walk with Him and become who you were created to be. He wants you to go all the way and experience the abundant, free life He died to give you!

That's why I'm so excited this journal is in your hands.

It means you're ready to let go of what's hindered you and move forward in faith. And I want to encourage you not to settle where you are today because moving forward feels uncomfortable. God said in Deuteronomy 30:19-20...

> ...I have set before you life and death, the blessing and the curse; therefore, you shall choose life in order that you may live, you and your descendants, by loving the LORD your God, by obeying His voice, and by holding closely to Him; for He is your life [your good life, your abundant life, your fulfillment]...

Those words were spoken by God to the Israelites as they were about to enter the Promised Land. But they also apply to us today.

As you listen to the CD teachings that accompany this journal, the statements, scriptures and action steps you find here will help you move forward in faith and take hold of everything Jesus gave His life for you to have. If you will make the decision to do whatever it takes to follow God's Word and be who He created you to be, there are no limits to what He will be able to do in you and through you.

Get ready to discover the abundant life Christ died to give you!

BELIEVE YOU CAN BEGIN AGAIN

"Don't listen to the lies of the enemy. You don't have to hide from God out of fear that He is angry or disappointed, and you don't have to find a way to move forward in your own strength. You can trust God to show you the way." —Joyce

Therefore let us [with privilege] approach the throne of grace [that is, the throne of God's gracious favor] with confidence and without fear, so that we may receive mercy [for our failures] and find [His amazing] grace to help in time of need [an appropriate blessing, coming just at the right moment] (Hebrews 4:16).

ACTION STEPS TO TAKE TODAY:

Take a moment right now and ask God to show you an area of your life where you need to believe you can begin again. Write it down and ask Him to show you what needs to change and how you can begin the process.

Find a passage of Scripture that speaks to you and memorize it. Write it down and put it on the fridge, on the dashboard of your car, or somewhere you'll see it every day, so it will be an encouragement to you often.

_____

_____

_____

_____

_____

_____

_____

_____

_____

_____

_____

_____

BELIEVE

BELIEVE

BELIEVE

BELIEVE

BELIEVE

LET GO OF THE PAST

"Don't focus on the mistakes of the past. Learn from them and move on. Never forget: You are a brand-new person in Christ!"   —Joyce

Therefore if anyone is in Christ [that is, grafted in, joined to Him by faith in Him as Savior], he is a new creature [reborn and renewed by the Holy Spirit]; the old things [the previous moral and spiritual condition] have passed away. Behold, new things have come [because spiritual awakening brings a new life] (2 Corinthians 5:17).

ACTION STEPS TO TAKE TODAY:

Instead of feeling condemned, learn from your past experiences and see God's grace in the midst of your mistakes. What would you do differently? What do you need to let go of today in order to move forward?

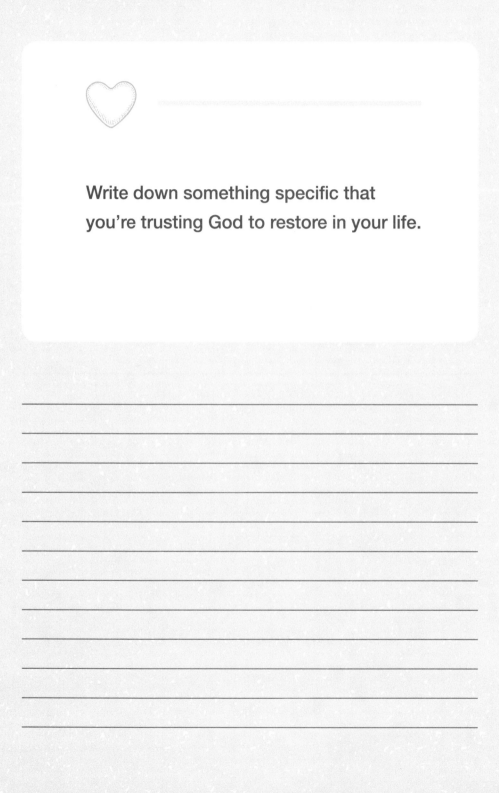

Write down something specific that
you're trusting God to restore in your life.

_____

_____

_____

_____

_____

_____

_____

_____

_____

_____

LET GO

LET GO

LET GO

LET GO

LET GO

REMEMBER YOUR NEW IDENTITY

"God wants to free you from the bondage of identity crisis and assure you of your identity in Him. He wants you to live a life full of joy, hope and purpose. That's His plan for you."   —Joyce

"'For I know the plans and thoughts that I have for you,' says the LORD, 'plans for peace and well-being and not for disaster, to give you a future and a hope'" (Jeremiah 29:11).

ACTION STEPS
TO TAKE TODAY:

What are some lies you have believed about yourself?

Now, write down the truth of what God's Word says. Remember, you have a new identity in Christ!

_____
_____
_____
_____
_____
_____
_____
_____
_____
_____
_____

IDENTITY

IDENTITY

IDENTITY

IDENTITY

IDENTITY

IDENTITY

4

LET GOD WORK

"With God, you always go forward... never backward. Forward into something new. Forward into something better. Forward into your destiny."   —Joyce

... But one thing I do: forgetting what lies behind and reaching forward to what lies ahead, I press on toward the goal to win the [heavenly] prize of the upward call of God in Christ Jesus (Philippians 3:13-14).

ACTION STEPS TO TAKE TODAY:

Is there something hindering you from being set free in your heart to move forward? Set aside some time today to pray and let God work in you. Write down what He shows you.

How is God calling you to move forward today?

_____

_____

_____

_____

_____

_____

_____

_____

_____

_____

_____

LET GOD

BE JOYFUL

"You don't have to be overcome and overwhelmed by the pressures of life. No matter how big your problem appears, you can defeat it with God's help and enjoy victory."   —Joyce

You will show me the path of life; in Your presence is fullness of joy; in Your right hand there are pleasures forevermore (Psalm 16:11).

ACTION STEPS TO TAKE TODAY:

What are some things that have a tendency to steal your joy?

What's a practical step you can take to be ready the next time the enemy attacks?

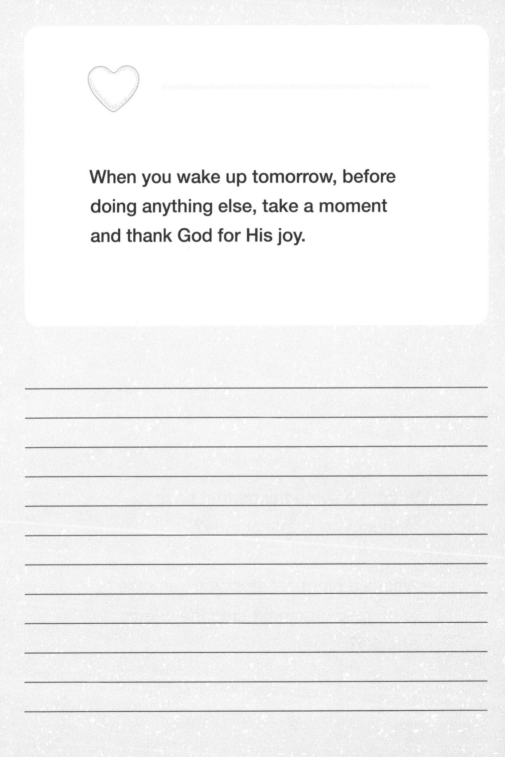

When you wake up tomorrow, before doing anything else, take a moment and thank God for His joy.

JOY

JOY

6

TAKE A STEP

"You'd be surprised at what God can do when you
are obedient with just one step. He can do more with
your one step than you ever thought possible. And, at
some point along the way, you'll look up and realize
you aren't walking anymore, you're running—running
into your destiny."   —Joyce

*"... Be strong and courageous! Do not be terrified or dismayed
(intimidated), for the LORD your God is with you wherever you go"*
(Joshua 1:9).

ACTION STEPS TO TAKE TODAY:

Don't let fear of doing the wrong thing keep you from taking action. In order to move forward, you need to take a step. Write down what God is showing you and one step you can take today.

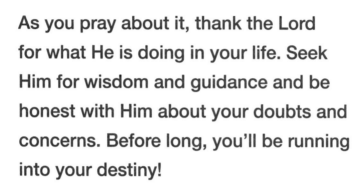

As you pray about it, thank the Lord for what He is doing in your life. Seek Him for wisdom and guidance and be honest with Him about your doubts and concerns. Before long, you'll be running into your destiny!

_____

_____

_____

_____

_____

_____

_____

_____

_____

_____

TAKE A STEP

TAKE A STEP

TAKE A STEP

LIVE IN REST

"Jesus came to give you a life full of peace and rest, a life full of joy in the Lord. Tired, run-down, worn-out lives are the old way of things. You don't have to live in that prison anymore; Jesus came to set you free!"   —Joyce

Therefore, while the promise of entering His rest still remains and is freely offered today, let us fear, in case any one of you may seem to come short of reaching it or think he has come too late (Hebrews 4:1).

ACTION STEPS TO TAKE TODAY:

Rest isn't wishful thinking—rest is the promise of God for your life. Whatever stresses or pressures you are going through today, you can cast those cares on the Lord and receive His rest (see Matthew 11:28-29; 1 Peter 5:6-7).

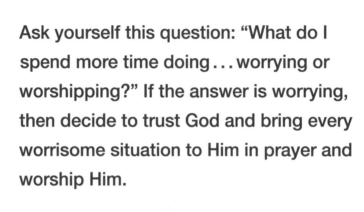

Ask yourself this question: "What do I spend more time doing...worrying or worshipping?" If the answer is worrying, then decide to trust God and bring every worrisome situation to Him in prayer and worship Him.

_____

_____

_____

_____

_____

_____

_____

_____

_____

_____

_____

8

HAVE A NEW ATTITUDE

"One of the things God showed me is that attitude is a result of perspective. How I choose to view a situation determines how I respond to it."   —Joyce

And we know [with great confidence] that God [who is deeply concerned about us] causes all things to work together [as a plan] for good for those who love God, to those who are called according to His plan and purpose (Romans 8:28).

ACTION STEPS TO TAKE TODAY:

Your attitude belongs to you, and nobody can force you to have a bad one if you refuse to do so. Make the decision to have a good one today.

Your perspective determines your attitude . . .

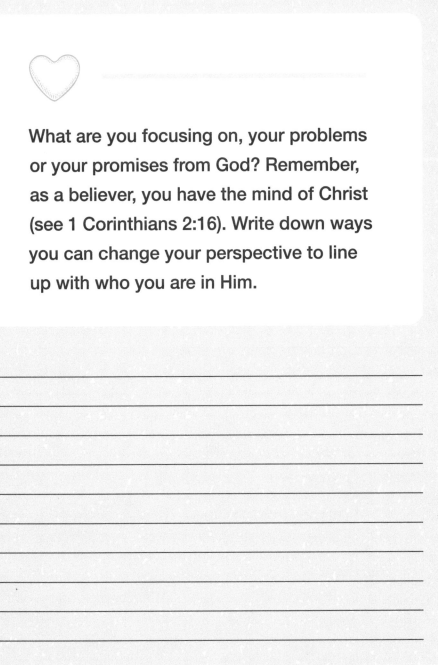

What are you focusing on, your problems or your promises from God? Remember, as a believer, you have the mind of Christ (see 1 Corinthians 2:16). Write down ways you can change your perspective to line up with who you are in Him.

_____

_____

_____

_____

_____

_____

_____

_____

_____

_____

ATTITUDE

ATTITUDE

ATTITUDE

ATTITUDE

ATTITUDE

ATTITUDE

9

SPEAK LIFE

"The words you say are setting the course for your life. The words you speak have the power to affect your joy, your prayers, and your future."   —Joyce

Death and life are in the power of the tongue, and those who love it and indulge it will eat its fruit and bear the consequences of their words (Proverbs 18:21).

ACTION STEPS TO TAKE TODAY:

Positive, faith-filled words will undo the results of the negative, complaining, and fearful words that you have spoken in the past. The moment you begin to speak God's Word over your life and get in agreement with Him by speaking faith into your situations, things will begin to change in your soul, and over time, you'll see changes in your circumstances.

What are some changes you can make regarding the words you speak? Find God's promises for your life in the Bible. Write them down and speak them out loud every day.

_____

_____

_____

_____

_____

_____

_____

_____

_____

SPEAK LIFE

SPEAK LIFE

_____

_____

_____

_____

_____

_____

_____

_____

_____

_____

_____

_____

_____

_____

_____

_____

_____

_____

_____

_____

_____

_____

_____

SPEAK LIFE

SPEAK LIFE

10

NEVER GIVE UP!

"You can overcome every obstacle, as long as you refuse to give up, because you have the Spirit of God inside of you."   —Joyce

Let us not grow weary or become discouraged in doing good, for at the proper time we will reap, if we do not give in (Galatians 6:9).

ACTION STEPS TO TAKE TODAY:

Perseverance is never about self-confidence and willpower based on your own strength; it is always about God-confidence and trusting that in Him, you can do whatever you need to do.

The Bible reminds us that God goes before us and that He wants to fight our battles for us.

Ask God to help you keep your focus on Him and remain determined to never give up. Write down what the Lord is showing you about His love and care for you, and believe Him for the victory!

_____

_____

_____

_____

_____

_____

_____

_____

_____

_____

PERSEVERANCE

PERSEVERANCE

PERSEVERANCE

PERSEVERANCE

PERSEVERANCE

PERSEVERANCE